What an Adventure!

by Jessica Quilty

Editorial Offices: Glenview, Illinois • Parsippany, New Jersey • New York, New York
Sales Offices: Needham, Massachusetts • Duluth, Georgia • Glenview, Illinois
Coppell, Texas • Ontario, California • Mesa, Arizona

Do you like adventure? Maybe you like to go hiking. Maybe you've climbed hills. Have you ever wondered what it would be like to go exploring with your friends?

Exploring a forest trail

Maybe you would like to join an outdoor adventure club. In this kind of club you can learn about nature. You can learn how to work as part of a team. You can make new friends!

Making new friends ⟹

In an adventure club you might go camping. You will learn how to use all kinds of outdoor tools. The picture below shows some of the things you might use.

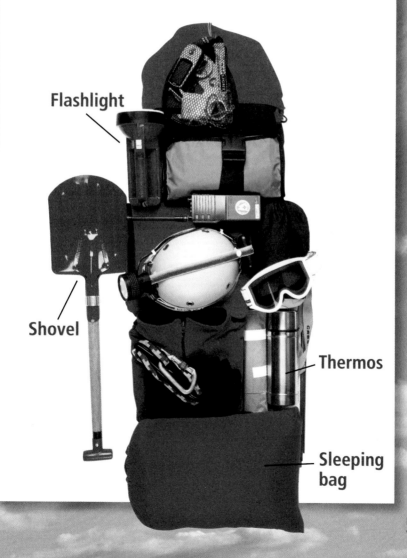

Flashlight

Shovel

Thermos

Sleeping bag

There are many exciting places to visit. You might visit the mountains. You might go canoeing down a cool river. Canoeing needs teamwork. Everyone in the canoe needs to paddle together.

You could go sailing on a lake. Sailing is not always easy. But it is a lot of fun! A sailboat has many ropes and other parts. You need to work with a friend to learn how to use them all.

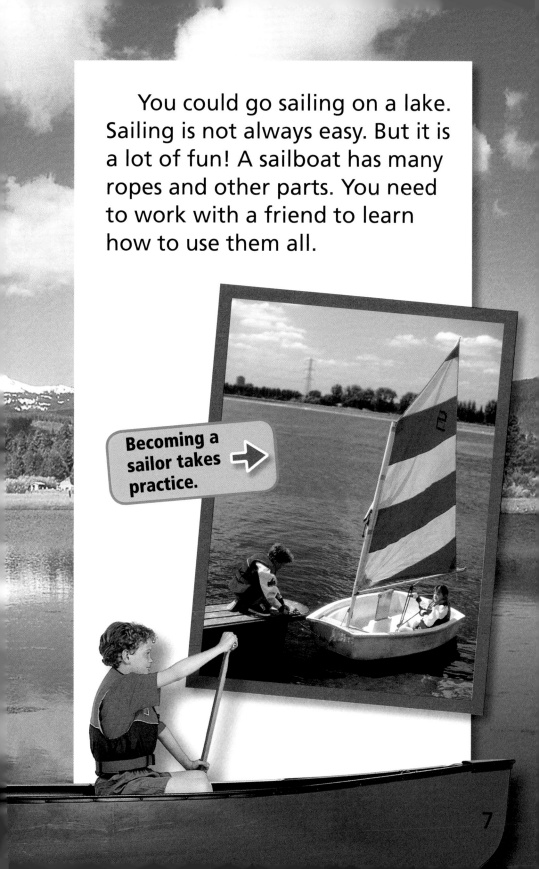

Becoming a sailor takes practice.

Some adventure clubs might take you on trips to the desert. You can explore lakes and rivers. You can learn all about desert plants and animals. You might go white water rafting.

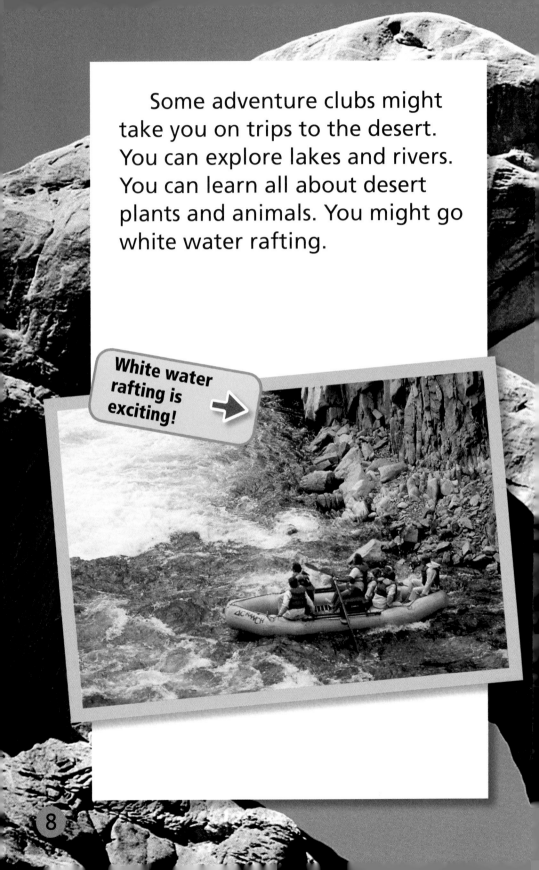

White water rafting is exciting!

People on teams help each other. Sometimes you will learn something fast. Then you can teach your friends. Other times your friends might teach you.

Learning how to fish is fun!

Some city adventure groups meet in clubhouses. You can work with other kids to learn about your city. You might help paint a mural or plant a community garden.

A city mural painted by kids

Joining an adventure club could be the greatest thing you ever did! The new skills you learn will stay with you forever.

Exploring a canyon

You could meet your truest friends in an adventure club. You will learn and laugh together. You will work hard as a team. Are you ready to start an adventure?

True friends camping